Putting on the
BRAKES

Young People's Guide to Understanding Attention Deficit Hyperactivity Disorder

REVISED EDITION

by Patricia O. Quinn, M.D.
and Judith M. Stern, M.A.

MAGINATION PRESS • WASHINGTON, DC

To our families:
Joe, Joseph, Timothy, Patrick, and Tara
Uzi, Talia, and Naomi

Published by
M A G I N A T I O N   P R E S S
An Educational Publishing Foundation Book
American Psychological Association
750 First Street, NE
Washington, DC 20002

For more information about our books, including a complete catalog, please write
to us, call 1-800-374-2721, or visit our website at www.maginationpress.com.

Library of Congress Cataloging-in-Publication Data

Quinn, Patricia O.
Putting on the brakes : young people's guide to understanding attention deficit
    hyperactivity disorder / Patricia O. Quinn and Judith Stern. — Rev. ed.
        p. ; cm.
Includes bibliographical references.
ISBN 1-55798-795-5 (softcover : alk. paper)
ISBN 1-55798-832-3 (hardcover : alk. paper)
1. Attention-deficit hyperactivity disorder — Treatment — Juvenile literature.
2. Cognitive therapy for children — Juvenile literature. [1. Attention-deficit
    hyperactivity disorder.] I. Stern, Judith M. II. Title.

RJ496.A86 Q56 2001
618.92'8589—dc21   2001030984

Manufactured in the United States of America
10 9 8 7 6 5

Contents

FOREWORD
To Parents and Professionals

When young people learn they have an attention disorder (AD/HD*), they have many questions, doubts, and fears. This book, written from the perspective of a pediatrician and an educator, addresses their needs and questions. School-age children respect material they find in a book, especially when it confirms or elaborates what they have learned from experience or from a significant adult. Children need reassurance that the problems they have are not unique to them. They benefit from a sense that help is available and that they themselves can be a powerful force in their own treatment.

Putting on the Brakes attempts to give children with AD/HD a sense of control and a perception of obtainable goals. This revised and expanded edition includes the significant advances that have been made in the treatment and understanding of AD/HD since publication of the first edition ten years ago. However, it is not meant to replace professional guidance and consultation, which should be an ongoing process in the lives of children diagnosed with AD/HD.

*In order to include all children with a diagnosed attention disorder, we use the term AD/HD to represent all three of the subtypes currently identified by professionals in the field: the inattention/distractible subtype, the hyperactive/impulsive subtype, and the combined subtype involving features of both. By using this terminology, we hope to minimize confusion and to avoid distinctions that are more appropriate for diagnostic classification than for children coping with this disorder.

The book was designed to be used with young people between the ages of 8 and 13. By reading the book together with their child, parents may begin an ongoing discussion that will provide information and reassurance. It is important to keep the hopeful message of this book in mind while reading and talking together with children. Depending on reading ability, the book may be read by the child alone or out loud by an adult. Efforts have been made to explain unfamiliar or difficult words. A glossary has been provided at the back so that the reader may conveniently look up any unfamiliar words as often as necessary.

In order to avoid overwhelming the child with too much information all at once, it is recommended that the book be read and discussed in sections. By providing frequent opportunities to discuss the contents of each page, an adult can help the child manage what is being covered. These discussions can be used to clear up misunderstandings, share personal insights, or raise further questions.

Children should be encouraged to read the book a number of times, as they may absorb additional meaning each time. The book might also be shared with siblings and friends, with the guidance of an informed adult.

Teachers and counselors may find this book and its companion activity books useful in helping children better understand their AD/HD and its impact on their lives. These books may also be used by professionals when working with a small group of children who are engaged in the process of learning about their attention disorder.

Part 1

Understanding AD/HD

What Is AD/HD All About?

How Do You Know If You Have AD/HD?

Are You the Only One With AD/HD?

What Is Going On in the Brain?

What Are You Feeling?

1

What Is AD/HD All About?

Imagine a sleek red sports car driving around a track. It's flying down the stretches, speeding around the curves, smooth and low to the road, the engine racing...BUT... it has no brakes. It can't stop when the driver wants it to stop. It can't slow down to a safer speed. It may get off the track, or even crash! It will certainly have a hard

time proving to everyone what it really can do.

If you have an attention deficit disorder, you may be like that racing car. You have a good engine (with lots of thinking power) and a good strong body, but your brakes don't work very well. You might not be able to keep still or stop yourself from doing something, even when you know you should.

What Is AD/HD?

Not everyone with an attention disorder is exactly the same. They may have any or all of the following problems:

- Trouble paying attention
- Trouble focusing on just one thing at a time
- Trouble keeping still
- Trouble thinking before acting
- Trouble keeping track of things
- Trouble learning in school

Experts who work with children with attention disorders have names for the different types, depending on which of these problems are causing the most trouble.

1. One type of attention disorder describes children who mainly have difficulty paying attention (**inattention**) and focusing (**distractibility**).
2. Another type includes children who have more difficulty with keeping still when they need to (**hyperactivity**) and who frequently act before they think things through (**impulsivity**).
3. Many children with attention disorders have a **combination** of all of these problems.

You have probably seen and heard different names and initials used to describe these different types of attention problems. ADD, ADHD, and AD/HD are the most common. In this book, we use the term AD/HD to include all of the types. No matter which of the types describes you, this book will help you better understand and take control of your AD/HD.

The following pages describe in more detail some of the problems that young people with AD/HD may face. As you are reading, see if any of these problems sound familiar to you.

Trouble Paying Attention (Inattention)

If you have trouble staying tuned in or paying attention to any one thing for more than a few minutes, you have a short attention span. This is where the first part of the name AD/HD comes from: **attention deficit** hyperactivity disorder.

Difficulty with paying attention affects many things. It may take you longer to start or finish assignments. At home or school, it may be difficult to pay attention to directions so you know what you should be doing. When talking with others or during class discussion, you may lose track of what is being said.

We all find it easier to concentrate when we are interested in something, so paying attention may not be a problem when you are doing something that you like. You may find it much easier to pay attention when the subject interests you, but feel quite lost when the topic is difficult or uninteresting. Your parents and teachers may be confused by this and think you should be able to pay attention all the time.

You may get angry when an adult keeps telling you to pay attention, especially when you feel that you are trying very hard to do just that. And in spite of your efforts, the results may not be as good as you (or your parents or teachers) wish.

14

Trouble Focusing on Just One Thing (Distractibility)

Kids with AD/HD have more trouble than others focusing on just one thing. Thoughts, ideas, sights, and sounds keep interrupting their train of thought.

When you are taking a math test, other thoughts may interfere and keep you from concentrating on the test. It may be hard to listen to your teacher when you find so many other things to look at or listen to in the classroom. You may be playing with the pencil on your desk or watching the man mowing the lawn outside, instead of focusing on the lesson. A bird singing outside the window may keep you from hearing the teacher give a homework assignment.

Kids say it's like switching channels on a TV and not being able to stay tuned in to one channel. Because of this difficulty focusing, you sometimes miss what is going on. When many different thoughts keep popping into your head, one right after the other, they interfere with what you are trying to do.

Trouble Keeping Still (Hyperactivity)

If you are hyperactive, it may be difficult for you to keep still. You always have to be moving. Sitting in one place is especially hard and may make you feel very restless. You feel that you have to stand up, fidget, or move around. Not being able to move may make you feel upset, tired, or sleepy. Some hyperactive children seem to talk all the time without giving other people a turn.

It is frustrating to be told over and over to stop moving, or to sit still. Like the racecar that doesn't have any brakes, you have difficulty stopping even when you want to stop.

16

Trouble Thinking Before Acting (Impulsivity)

Sometimes you may do or say things without thinking. You may ride your bicycle through your mother's garden, or call out the answer in class without raising your hand, or start a test before all the directions are explained. You may interrupt others, or say the first thing that comes into your head, whatever it is!

Doing or saying something without thinking—with no brakes to stop you — is called impulsive behavior.

People may ask, "Why did you do that?" At that moment, you may not know why, so you'll say, "I don't know." After some thought, you may be able to discuss what you did wrong.

However, you may still forget to "think before you act" the next time. This can be very frustrating for both you and the people around you.

Trouble Keeping Track of Things (Disorganization)

Kids with AD/HD may be very disorganized. Keeping track of belongings, school assignments, or chores may be a problem. You may forget or lose things more than other people do. You may not know how to keep track of time or how to manage it well. In the morning, you may suddenly discover you have run out of time. The bus has arrived, and you are not ready.

You may postpone school assignments until the last minute and then have to rush. The work you turn in may not show all you really know. You might have done better if you had started earlier. You may then feel disappointed when you get your assignment back with many corrections, knowing that you could have done better.

Putting on the
BRAKES

Trouble Learning in School (Learning Difficulties)

Because of all these problems, children with AD/HD may have trouble in school. You may need extra help, but you are just as smart as other kids. You may need a tutor to keep you organized or help you with your work.

Some children with AD/HD also have a learning disability in a subject area such as reading, math, or written language. This means that they are learning significantly below what is expected for their intelligence and grade level. If a child with AD/HD also has a learning disability, he or she may work with a learning specialist to make progress in the subject area that is causing trouble.

Most kids with AD/HD have lots of questions.

Why can I pay attention better on certain days?
Am I the only one with this problem?
How do I know if I have AD/HD?
Is there something wrong with my brain?
Why am I like this?

This book will try to answer your questions.

How Do You Know If You Have AD/HD?

Everyone has some of the problems we have discussed some of the time. It can be hard to pay attention in school when you are thinking about your birthday party that afternoon or about a new baby sister at home. If something very serious happens, such as a divorce or death in the family, worry or depression may cause a person to be restless, irritable,or forgetful, or have trouble paying attention.

However, if you have attention problems for a long time and they are not related to a stressful situation, you may have AD/HD. Deciding if you have AD/HD can be done only by professionals who are experts in this area. These experts may include pediatricians, psychologists, psychiatrists, and neurologists—different kinds of doctors who know all about AD/HD and can help children who have it.

During an evaluation for AD/HD, you may be seen by a doctor and tested on how you learn and on your ability to concentrate. You may visit with more than one kind of doctor. These professionals will also talk to your parents and teachers and may ask them to fill out forms that ask questions about you and what you are like at home and at school. These forms help your teachers and parents report on the areas of behavior, attention, and learning that might be problems for you. After gathering all this information, the experts can decide if your problems are the result of AD/HD.

Are You the Only One With AD/HD?

Can you guess who in this class has AD/HD?

You can't tell, because kids with AD/HD look just like everybody else!

About one in every 20 children has a problem with attention that affects their learning or behavior. As many as 2.5 million school-age children in the United States are thought to have AD/HD. A class of 20 might have one or two children with some form of AD/HD. Both boys and girls can have AD/HD.

You may not be able to point out these children very easily, because they look just like everybody else. People often expect that kids with AD/HD are easy to spot because of their hyperactivity. But we now know that not all kids with AD/HD are hyperactive, so they may be more difficult to identify.

Although you may feel a little different from the other kids in your class, you have lots of company when you consider how many other children your age have this problem!

What Is Going On in the Brain?

The brain is made up of several areas, each with its own specific job. The outside layers of the brain are called the **cerebral cortex**. This is the part of the brain where most thinking and learning takes place. It is also where memories are stored.

Under the cortex is an area called the **subcortex**. The subcortex is an important part of the braking system that helps control both your attention and your activity level. This area contains the **relay system**, which has many jobs: It takes information coming in and decides where it should go, it decides what you should pay attention to at the time, and it sends messages to "turn on" other parts of the brain. The subcortex also helps us stay alert and coordinates our brain's activities.

The brain is made up of many cells called **neurons**. These cells work together but do not actually touch each other. They are separated by a tiny space called a **synapse**. The neurons relay information or messages to each other by sending a chemical messenger across this space. These messengers are called **neurotransmitters**.

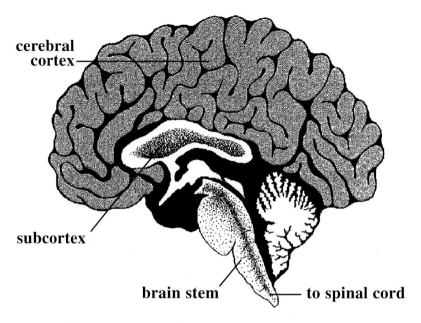

cerebral cortex

subcortex

brain stem — **to spinal cord**

For the neuron to relay the message to the cells around it, there must be enough of the messenger to do the job, and the messenger must stay in the space (synapse) long enough to join with a **receptor** on each of the surrounding cells. This joining of the neurotransmitter to the receptor is like a key fitting into a lock. When the neurotransmitter (key) fits into the receptor (lock), it opens the door for messages to get through.

When the brain is working properly, there is enough neurotransmitter to turn on the cells and deliver the messages where they are supposed to go. In the brain of a person with AD/HD, this may not always be happening. Messages to put on the brakes, to slow down, and to pay attention may not be getting through effectively. A person may then act without thinking (impulsivity) or be very distracted by other things.

Scientists have several explanations for why the messages are poorly transmitted when someone has AD/HD. When scientists take pictures of the brain (called scans) in people with AD/HD, they find that the areas that control attention and help with planning ahead are not working properly. It seems that there is not enough of the neurotransmitter to turn on the neurons in these areas and to keep them turned on.

Scientists have also recently found that there is a system in each cell that takes the neurotransmitter from the synapse and carries it back inside the cell that first sent it out. This is called the **transporter system**. It seems that some people with AD/HD have too many of these transporters. This causes the neurotransmitter to be taken back into the cell before it can relay the message to nearby cells. When this happens, other areas of the brain cannot do their job. This may help explain why kids with AD/HD have trouble paying attention or getting organized. It's why they forget or lose things, or why they act as if they have no brakes.

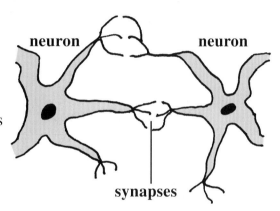

Scientists also know that while these problems with the neurotransmitters affect some of the brain's jobs like learning and remembering, they do not affect intelligence, personality, or creativity. Kids with AD/HD are just as smart, talented, and healthy as other children.

5

What Are You Feeling?

Kids with AD/HD have lots of different thoughts and feelings. Sometimes they feel:

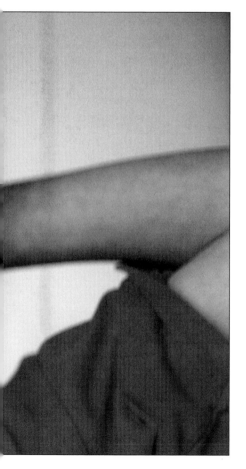

Confused   **Impatient**   **Dumb**

Overloaded

Restless   **Scared**

Angry   **Frustrated**

Misunderstood

Teased   **Tense**

Anxious   **Picked on**

Unpopular

Lost   **Forgetful**

What feelings do you have?

Let's look at some of these feelings:

- You may feel **confused** or **lost** if you tune out and miss important pieces of information. Even if you look and listen carefully, some of the information just never seems to get into your brain.

- You may feel **overloaded** if too much information comes in at one time.

- You may feel **restless** when you have to sit still.

- You may feel **impatient** and find that it's hard to wait. You may call out answers in class or have trouble waiting for your turn in a game. If you are impulsive, you start things before you fully understand what to do. You may rush through assignments at school without checking them afterward. This may result in many careless errors and low grades. You may feel **frustrated** and **angry** because you really knew the right answer.

- You may find it hard to study and take tests. Even

when you review the material ahead of time, the information somehow "disappears" by the time the test begins. Then you may feel **forgetful** and **dumb**.

- If this happens often, you may feel **scared** or **anxious** when you know you have a test coming up. When you feel **tense**, it is even harder for you to pay attention.

- You may feel **picked on** if your parents scold or nag you more than they do your brothers or sisters. Your impulsive behaviors may sometimes be unsafe. You may need more reminders than other family members. Your parents care about your safety and happiness. They try to help you do the things they think are best for you, but this may sometimes feel like nagging.

- You may feel **unpopular**. If you often say or do things before you think, other kids might not want to be with you. If you cannot wait your turn or follow the rules when you are playing games, other kids may not want to be your friend. If you are messy or can never sit still, you may be **teased**. All this can make you feel **misunderstood**.

Now for the good news! Kids with AD/HD also feel:

Energetic	**Curious**	**Athletic**
Special	**Creative**	**Artistic**
Sensitive	**Humorous**	**Attractive**
Imaginative	**Smart**	**Enthusiastic**
Friendly	**Caring**	**Happy**

What are your feelings?

Along with all the problems of AD/HD, there are also some surprising gifts:

- You can use your **extra energy** and **enthusiasm** in many positive ways. You may love to run and jump, play sports, or dance. You may be very **athletic**, and people look up to you for that talent.

- You may be a very **creative** person and have many good ideas. Your **curiosity** and **imagination** may help you think and do things in ways that other people may truly admire.

- You may be **artistic**.

- You may have a good **sense of humor** and make other people laugh.

- You may be especially **sensitive** and **caring** and very aware of other people's feelings. You may like to help people and be extremely **friendly**.

And, of course, AD/HD kids are as **attractive, smart, special,** and even as **happy** as anyone else.

More Good News!

Because you have had to deal with the problems of AD/HD from an early age, you have a head start on other kids. You have the advantage of knowing your strengths and weaknesses. You are used to working hard to accomplish a goal. This ability to adapt and cope can be a real gift for you.

Now that you have learned more about AD/HD, the next part of the book will tell you some ways that you can put on the brakes and feel more in control of your life.

Part 2

Gaining Control

Getting Support

Making Friends

Understanding Medication

Becoming More Organized

CHAPTER

Getting Support

We all need people in our lives who are able to see what is special about us and give us help when things feel hard. Kids with AD/HD need support as well. It is important to know that you don't need to manage everything alone. There are many ways to find extra help.

Here are some of the ways kids with AD/HD have found support:

"My family helps me out by listening to my problems and working on homework with me."

"I call my grandmother in another city once a week. She is happy to hear about all the good things I've done and gives helpful advice when I have a problem."

"I go to the guidance counselor at school when I need to talk about problems I'm having or how I'm feeling."

"I meet in a group of kids with a therapist who helps us understand our problems and feel good about ourselves. Sometimes the therapist also works with our families to learn new ways to help us."

"I meet with my teacher at school several times a month to talk, get extra help with my work, and find out if I'm missing any assignments."

"My doctor helps me. She prescribes medication to help me concentrate and pay attention."

Your Support Team

When you have AD/HD, getting a little extra help can make a big difference. Sometimes, talking to a counselor or therapist will give you an opportunity to understand yourself better and think of ways to help yourself. Therapists can help with many things, such as controlling your anger, making friends, or learning how to deal with teasing. They may also make some suggestions on how to become better organized or how to do your homework in less time.

Counselors may also meet with your parents or teachers to provide them with ideas that will assist you at home or school. Some kids with AD/HD might meet with a counselor to learn how to get along with others.

Tutors and school resource teachers work with many students who have attention problems. They can provide suggestions for improving your organization skills, keeping up with homework, and learning how to follow directions. Since they work with you alone or in a small group, they really get to know you and figure out strategies that are designed to meet your unique needs.

Depending on your needs, there may be many people who are part of your support "team." These people might include your parents, teachers, counselor, tutors, coaches, therapist, and your doctor. They all do their part, but you are the most important part of this team. Your ideas, cooperation, and hard work all add up when it comes to making positive changes.

7

Making Friends

Now that you have learned more about AD/HD and understand yourself better, this may be a good time for you to begin working on making and keeping friends. Having more friends in your life will make you feel even better.

For some kids with AD/HD, making friends can be

difficult. If someone always wants things his way, has trouble waiting his turn, doesn't listen, or says and does things without thinking, other children may not want to be his friend. Some kids with AD/HD may have trouble knowing what to say or do to be part of a group. But with some extra work, most kids with AD/HD can learn how to be a good friend.

What Makes a Good Friend?

Let's think about what makes someone a good friend.
A friend:

- Shares some of your interests
- Shares toys, ideas, or activities
- Is kind and thoughtful
- Listens to what you say
- Is willing to wait her turn

Find someone in your class or neighborhood with whom you feel comfortable and who is interested in some of the same things that you are. Talk to that person and make plans to get together. When you are first getting to know each other, plan to be together for only a little while, until you learn more about each other.

For the first few times you get together, plan on doing an activity that you both like. This could be something like working on a craft project, riding bikes, playing ball, or going to a movie. If you are going to be playing a game, work together to make up the rules of a game before you start. Make sure you don't change them once the game begins.

Remember that not everything should always be done your way. Be flexible and try your friend's ideas some of the time.

If acting impulsively is a problem for you, try hard to slow down and think before acting. Take a minute to look at the situation, and try to think of two ways you could

respond. Choose the one that is "friendlier."

Good friends are kind and considerate. Make it a habit to say something nice about the other person each time you are together. When you are thoughtful of other people, you will be surprised by how often they are nice to you in return.

Some kids do better during planned group activities such as bowling, baseball, scouting, 4H, or other youth organizations. Other kids might do better playing at home with just one or two friends. Regardless of what works best for you, having an adult around to supervise can help keep things running smoothly. If something does go wrong, the adult is there to help you.

You can also discuss problems you are having in your friendships with your parents or counselor. With their help, try to come up with ideas and solutions. You could practice with them some ways to act differently next time.

Don't forget that any friendship can have difficult moments. Sometimes the best you can do is say you are sorry or stop doing what hurt the other person. That's not easy for anyone, but it can be the best way to keep a friendship going!

Understanding Medication

For some kids with AD/HD, the doctor may prescribe a stimulant medication to help with attention problems. Stimulant medication allows you to concentrate and pay better attention. This medicine is not given to you because you are sick. Instead, it is used to improve the way your brain functions.

Stimulants work by changing the levels of the neurotransmitters and making the receptors in the brain work more efficiently. This makes focusing, as well as learning, easier. Stimulants can also decrease impulsivity and help you manage your own behavior by keeping to the rules and doing what you know is right.

Stimulants have been used to treat AD/HD for a long time. There have been many, many research studies conducted to prove that they are safe and that they work to treat AD/HD, when used correctly.

Here are some of the things that other kids with AD/HD have said about taking medication to treat it:

"It helps me think one thought at a time."

"It's like glue. Before, my thoughts were all in pieces. The medicine stuck them all together."

"I feel more organized."

"It helps me calm down."

"It helps me not climb the walls or get into trouble."

"It helps me pay better attention."

"Before, my brain was cloudy, but now it's all cleared up."

"It lets me show how smart I am."

"It helps me get my work done."

"Thirty minutes after I take my medicine, the AD/HD just packs up and moves out."

"It's my memory and concentration pill."

"It is my brain-aid, just like a band-aid for my brain."

What You Need to Know

If your doctor has prescribed medicine for your AD/HD, it is important that you learn as much as you can about it, including its name, what it looks like, and the amount or dose you are supposed to take each time. This is all very important information.

You should never take a medicine when you don't know what it is, and you should only take medication from someone who is authorized to give it to you, such as the school nurse. You should never take anyone else's medication, ever.

Medication can help you to be more organized and focused. It can help you remember the rules at home and at school. It can help you be more in control over what you say and do. It can help you pay better attention during class and after-school activities.

But the medication can't do everything. You still have work to do, and members of your "team" can help you. For example, when you are taking your medication and are confronted by a bully, you may be better able to control yourself and stay out of a fight, but you may not know what to do instead. You still need to learn new behaviors. That's where working with someone else can help you come up with some more appropriate behaviors.

Also, medication may help you improve your concentration, but in order to do better in school, you may need to work with your teacher or tutor to learn more effective study skills. You still need to put in the time studying and doing all of your assignments, but things might go more smoothly now that you are more organized and better focused.

The Right Medication for You

AD/HD affects your life, all day, every day. Usually kids need to pay attention throughout the day – at school, at home, and during after-school activities, such as homework, sports, and music or dance lessons. It is important that you and your parents work with your doctor to find the right kind of medication and the right dose that helps you and lasts long enough for when you need it during the day.

Today, there are many medications available to treat AD/HD. These medicines can help you pay better attention at home and at school. With a range of medications available, you and your doctor have lots of options to choose from. Each child with AD/HD is unique. That means that certain medications are better at reducing their symptoms than others. You will need to work with your doctor to determine which type of medicine is best for you. The two most commonly prescribed stimulant medications are methylphenidate and the amphetamines.

Methylphenidate. Methylphenidate comes in short-, intermediate-, and long-acting pills. The most commonly used brand of the short-acting (lasts a few hours) stimulant is Ritalin. This medication usually starts working in about 20 minutes and lasts about 4 hours. If it is taken before school or early in the morning, its effects usually wear off by lunch. Your doctor might then recommend that you take another pill at lunchtime at school. Your parents and doctor may also want you to take a third dose of medication to help you with your homework and other after-school activities.

The intermediate-release versions of methylphenidate include Ritalin SR and Metadate. These last a little longer (up to 6 hours) and might allow you to get through the entire school day with one dose. After school you then might need to take a dose of a short-acting pill for after-school activities.

A long-acting version of methylphenidate, called Concerta, lasts about 12 hours. With this medicine, you take only one pill in the morning, and its effects last until the evening.

Amphetamines. The amphetamine most often prescribed is Dexedrine. This also comes in pills that are short- and longer-acting. The short-acting pills need to be taken two or three times a day.

Dexedrine is also available as longer-acting Dexedrine Spansules and as Adderall. For some kids, the longer-acting amphetamine pill may need to be taken only once in the morning, and its effects last through the school day. Depending on how long the effects last, a doctor may suggest that some kids take these pills two or even three times a day to last the entire day and into the evening when they usually do homework.

Side Effects

Some of these medicines may make you feel less hungry. This doesn't happen to everyone, but if it happens to you, it is important that you not lose weight. Eat a good breakfast, and try to eat something at lunchtime. You can also make up for lost calories by eating nutritious snacks

in the afternoon and before you go to bed at night.

A few kids complain about a slight stomachache after they take the medicine. Be sure to tell your parents, doctor, or teacher if you have that problem. Eating some crackers or drinking a glass of water will usually make the feeling go away.

You should also drink a full glass of water when taking the pill, instead of just a sip. That will sometimes prevent the ache from coming in the first place.

Amphetamines should not be taken with citrus drinks (orange, grapefruit, lemon, or lime), but you can take most of the stimulant medications before or after you eat without it making a difference.

Working Together With Your Doctor

Remember to tell your parents and doctor how you feel while you are taking the medicine so that they can help you. Visit your doctor and have a check-up regularly while you are taking your medicine. She or he can check your height, weight, and blood pressure, and do a blood test if needed to make sure you are healthy and growing well. People used to think that AD/HD medication would cause a slowdown in growth, but this has not been proven in studies that follow children for a long time.

All medicine needs to be prescribed and monitored closely by your doctor. Your doctor is the person in charge of your medicine. You should take only as much as your doctor prescribes. However, you are an important part of the plan to help you do well. Make sure all of your treatments are explained to you and that you understand them.

By following your progress closely, your doctor will be able to determine how much medicine you need and when you should take it. Sometimes it will be necessary to adjust the dose or change the medication until the best one can be found for you. But only you will know if the medicine is helping and when it wears off. You need to tell your doctor how you feel and make sure all of your opinions and questions are heard and answered.

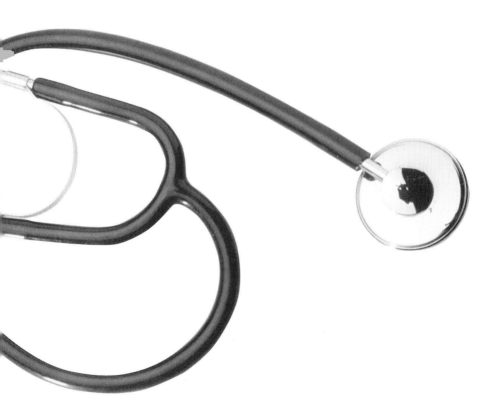

Becoming More Organized

There are many things you can do to become more in control of your life both at home and at school. Here are some of the concerns kids with AD/HD often have:

How can I become better at following directions?
How can I become a better listener?
How can I become better organized and not lose things?
How can I keep track of all the things I need to do?
How can I manage my time well?
How can I make my work look better and neater?
How can I stop being so messy?
How should I study for tests?

These questions are answered in the following sections.

Following Directions

When you cannot remember everything that your teacher tells you to do, try writing a few **key words** while the teacher is speaking. For example, your teacher is telling you about tomorrow's assignment. She says, "The work must be written in cursive. It should be at least two paragraphs long. Be sure to use correct quotation marks." You can jot down a few reminder notes to look at when you get home. The notes might look like this:

1. cursive
2. 2 paragraphs
3. use quotation marks

Let's try another one. Your math teacher says, "Open to page 39 in your book. Do section B in class now and section C tonight for homework. Remember to use pencil and graph paper." Your notes might look like this:

Math Homework
1. page 39
2. section C
3. pencil
4. graph paper

If it is difficult for you to write words, try making a few **quick pictures** to help you remember something. Your mother says, "After dinner, feed the dog. Then clean up your desk." You can make drawings like these:

Let's try another one. Your physical education teacher says, "Bring in your sneakers and shorts for gym tomorrow." Here is an example of some drawings:

You may need to remind adults (parents, teachers, coaches) that it is hard for you to remember a lot of information when you are only hearing it. Perhaps they can write the information down for you. Or a classmate who writes quickly could make some notes for you. Who do you know like that? See if you can work out an arrangement with them, or ask your teacher to find someone who is a fast note-taker.

Managing Your Time

If you have trouble keeping track of time, use clocks, timers, and calendars to help. Before you start a task, take a guess at how long you think it will take to complete. Then **time yourself** and compare this time with your first guess. With practice, you will get better at figuring out how long things take. You can keep a record of your progress on a piece of paper or the computer.

Project	Amount of Time:	
	Guess	Actual
1. Math homework	40 minutes	20 minutes
2. Proofread book report	10 minutes	30 minutes
3. Complete spelling sentences	45 minutes	40 minutes
4. Clean backpack	2 minutes	20 minutes

Another idea is to **use a timer or an alarm** when you know you have only a certain amount of time to do something. This can help you to stay focused rather than get sidetracked. If you have a watch with an alarm, you can set it to go off at the time you want to be finished, or set it a few minutes before you need to stop.

When you have lots of different things to do, it usually helps to **make a list**. Here are some different kinds of lists that come in handy.

Things to Do Today
1. *Get permission slip signed.*
2. *Study for spelling test.*
3. *Practice part for the play.*
4. *Two pages in language workbook.*
5. *Clean hamster cage.*

Other Things for This Week — *Date Due*

1. *Current events assignment* — *Nov. 7*
2. *Social studies test* — *Nov. 8*
3. *Note cards for science report due* — *Nov. 9*

Reports Projects Due After This Week

Date Due

1. Return health survey   Nov. 14
2. Collage for art   Nov. 16
3. Social studies report   Dec. 1

Once you have written down these due dates, you will not have to worry about remembering them in your head. Make sure to keep this information in a place where you can check it every day. Large wall calendars work well. You can use them to **record the due dates**.

When you have a large assignment such as a research report, a big test, or a science fair project coming up, you can **break down the assignment into smaller steps** you need to follow. Then write each of these steps on a separate calendar day so you will know what to do each day. Some examples might be:

SUNDAY	MONDAY	TUESDAY	WEDNESDAY	THURSDAY	FRIDAY	SATURDAY
		1	2	3 *Read Chapter 4 of biography*	4	5
6	7	8 *Work on science fair project 25 minutes*	9	10	11	12
13	14	15	16	17	18	19

Try to **spread out** what you have to do so that no day becomes overloaded. It may be helpful to have a parent, teacher, tutor, or counselor work with you to show you how to pace yourself and how to break big jobs down into smaller parts.

Here is something important to remember about managing time. Things often take longer to do than we think they will, or something unexpected happens (a relative comes to visit, you get sick) that changes your original plan. So it's a good idea to **build extra time into your plans**. If you think something you've never done before is going to take 15 minutes, allow yourself 30 minutes. Or when planning a big assignment, plan to finish it a few days before it is due, just in case you do need some extra time toward the end.

Some students like to make their **running reminder lists** on the computer, so they can add or take away items

easily. Wipe off boards and blackboards are also easy to use, since you can erase things as they are completed, and add others that you need to remember.

Small electronic devices that fit in your pocket or backpack can be purchased. Once you learn to use them, they are great for storing lots of information: due dates, test dates, assignments, and special events. Since they are expensive and easy to lose, you may have to plan with your parents when you will be ready to own and use one.

Keeping Up With Homework

Homework assignment books can help keep you on track when used correctly. Make sure to write down all of your assignments each day. Don't rely on your memory.

Check your assignment book each day before leaving school, so you know what you will need to bring home that day. When you get home, review all that you need to do that day, so you can make a homework plan for the day. A parent or babysitter can help you with this.

If your school requires you to use a specific assignment book, learn how to use it at the beginning of the year. If the spaces are small, decide where you will write additional homework notes and reminders to yourself. If you are allowed to choose your own assignment book, you and a parent should look for one that is well organized and gives you plenty of room to write.

Organizing Your Things

If you have a messy bedroom, school desk, locker, or backpack, enlisting the help of an adult might help you to develop a better system.

One idea some kids with AD/HD find useful is to put many **shelves** into their closet or on their wall. Each shelf can be marked with the name of a particular item or group of items. Using plastic baskets can also help you organize some of your things.

Colors can help with your organization. For example, you might put all math work in a red folder and history in a green folder. Or at home, you might put underwear in a drawer with a yellow sticker, shirts in a drawer with a blue sticker, and socks in a drawer with a red sticker.

Choose a **specific day and time** each week for cleaning out your backpack or desk. You might want to get an adult to help you with this, too.

Try keeping a **box near the front door** of your house. You can use it for your schoolbooks when you come home. You can take the books out to do homework, but put them back when you are finished. You can also put in anything you need for school the next day, such as your gym clothes or a permission slip for a class trip. Everything will be in one place when you are ready to leave in the morning. This will help you be more organized each day.

Improving Study Habits

There are many different ways to study. Some kids with AD/HD learn better when they **review** or **discuss** material with a friend, parent, or tutor. This gives students a chance to repeat information so they will remember it better. It also allows them to ask questions if there is something they are not sure about.

Another study strategy is to **underline** or **highlight** the most important information to be studied. When you do this, you are able to focus on only the material you need to know, instead of paying attention to the extra, less important information.

Some students study alone using a **tape recorder**, reading the most important points from notes or the book. They listen to the recorded notes over and over. This works well for kids who need to hear things several times in order to really learn them. Also, when you speak into the tape recorder, you are saying the information in a way that you can understand it.

Students who get restless easily sometimes find that **moving around** while they study is helpful. This helps get rid of some of your extra energy, which may then make it easier for you to concentrate. Try walking as you read or pedal an exercise bicycle, if there is one in your house. Another idea is to exercise before you begin your studying. This may help you feel more relaxed when you get started.

Kids who have trouble concentrating sometimes need to find a **quiet study place** that has very few distractions. Think of a place where you can focus best, and try to study there.

When you concentrate hard, you may need to take **regular short breaks** so that you don't start to feel sleepy or bored. Walk around, play a short game of catch, or go get a healthy snack. The change and movement will help you get back to work with improved focus.

Try studying in **different places or positions**. Try different techniques for studying, even those you had never considered before. The purpose of these efforts is to help you figure out the ways that work best for you. Some kids have a few ways that they study best. Other kids find that one way or one place works best. Get to know what works for you, and experiment with some new ways every once in awhile. As you get older, you may discover new techniques as well.

Improving Schoolwork

Some kids find it useful to sit near the **front of the class-room** in order to decrease distractions.

Some teachers may help kids focus on their work by giving them a **pre-arranged secret signal** to remind them to get back on track. Some examples include the teacher tapping her desk or holding a special pencil. You can come up with your own idea if the teacher agrees.

Before you pick up your pencil to do your work, it is a good idea to **read all the directions at least two times**. In this way, you will make sure to do the right thing from the start.

It is important that you **check over your class work and homework**. You want your teachers to see how much you really know, so show them work without careless errors.

Improving Proofreading

Look for mistakes in spelling, punctuation, and capitalization.

Check to see if all your sentences are complete and make sense. Read what you wrote out loud as a way of making sure that the sentences say what you meant.

Read your paper from the **bottom up**. This may help you spot your spelling and punctuation errors more easily.

Make a **game** of it. See how many mistakes you can find in five minutes. Exchange papers with a friend and look for errors in each other's work.

Use the **computer** for long homework assignments. Your work will look better, and you will find it easier to spot mistakes.

Use the **spell-check program** on your computer. You can also buy a small portable spell-check or a small dictionary, which you can use in school.

Improving Test Results

Study for each test over a period of many days. This makes it easier to review, and you will feel less nervous. As you begin a test, take a **deep breath** and remind yourself that you are prepared!

Don't pick up that pencil to start the test until you have **read all of the directions at least two times. Check the clock** a few times (or bring a watch) so that you make sure you are using your time well.

Keep a few pieces of **clean paper** on your desk when you take a test. If you find it hard to remember information, use the blank paper to jot down everything that does come into your head about the subject. This often helps bring back to mind the material you studied.

When you take an essay test, **write notes** on the paper, reminding yourself what you want to be sure to include in your answer. Once you begin the essay, you can always look back and not worry about forgetting an important point.

Always **check over** a test paper completely before you hand it in. Wait a few minutes and then **check it again.**

When you get back a graded test, take some time to **look it over.** See what you did well, and what you need to improve next time.

To the Boy or Girl With AD/HD

We hope you now know more about taking control of your life and about how to put on the brakes.

You have taken a big step by reading this book and learning what attention deficit disorders are all about. You can use this knowledge to make many positive changes in your life. Having AD/HD will not stop you from doing most things you want to do.

Reread any section of this book when you need it. You will continue to get ideas.

Encourage the people in your life (such as parents, sisters, brothers, other relatives, teachers, friends, and classmates) to read this book and to learn more about AD/HD and you.

Ask for help when you need it. There are many people who are willing to help you. With your cooperation, everyone can work together as a true team.

With hard work and a strong will, you can succeed. It is important to remember that although the suggestions in this book may seem like extra work, they are worth trying. Many AD/HD kids have found them helpful at home, at school, and with all the people in their lives.

It helps to have someone else work with you on trying out new ideas. Be creative. Experiment. See what works for you and use it! You really can change and improve.

Your attention disorder is just one part of you. Try hard to manage it, and you will have plenty of energy left over to enjoy the many other parts of life as well.

Best wishes,
Patricia 0. Quinn, M.D.
Judith M. Stern, M.A.

Amphetamine. A type of medication used to treat AD/HD that belongs to the stimulant class.

Attention Deficit Hyperactivity Disorder. A condition in a person of average or above-average intelligence that includes symptoms such as short attention span, distractibility, impulsivity, and/or hyperactivity.

Blood Pressure. The pressure of the blood against the inner walls of the blood vessels. It can be measured by a cuff placed around the upper arm.

Brain. The major organ of the nervous system. It controls all mental and physical activities.

Brain Stem. A part of the brain that controls automatic functions such as breathing, heart rate, and blood pressure.

Cerebellum. A part of the brain that controls the movements of the muscles, helps with balance, and controls attention.

Cerebral Cortex. The outermost layer of the brain. Its networks are essential to higher thinking activities such as memory and organizing information. It makes up 40% of total brain weight.

Conscious. A state of being awake and aware of what is going on around you.

Counselor. A professional who works with children or adults to help them understand feelings and solve their problems. Counselors may work in schools or have offices in other places.

Depression. Feeling sad and hopeless for a long time.

Diagnosis. Technical identification and description of a condition or problem.

Disorganization. Difficulty keeping track of materials and/or time.

Distractibility. Trouble staying focused on just one thing.

Dose. The correct amount of medicine a person needs to take at one time for the medicine to work properly.

Due Date. The date on which an assignment or project needs to be handed in.

Evaluation. Testing to determine how someone is functioning, or to find out if a person has a problem in one or more areas.

Hyperactivity. Excessive motor movements.

Impulsivity. Acting or speaking without thinking.

Irritable. Overly sensitive or in a bad mood.

Key Words. The most important words, such as a few words you would use to identify an assignment or remind yourself to do something.

Learning Disabilities. Significant difficulties in learning to read, write, or do mathematics that cause problems in school achievement.

Learning Specialist. A teacher who has special training in working with students who have learning difficulties.

Medication. Substances used to treat illnesses or to improve functioning of the body or brain. Current medications used for AD/HD most often are methylphenidate and amphetamines, with brand names such as Ritalin, Dexedrine, Concerta, Adderall, Metadate, and Clonidine.

Methylphenidate. A type of medication used to treat AD/HD that belongs to the stimulant class.

Neurologist. A medical doctor who is a specialist in the way the nervous system works. The nervous system of the body is made up of the brain, spinal cord, and nerves.

Neuron. A single brain cell.

Neurotransmitters. Chemical substances produced by brain cells (neurons) that act as messengers. They cross the space (synapse) between cells and carry information to other brain cells.

Organized. Being able to put things in their correct order or place.

Pediatrician. A medical doctor who is a specialist in the health of children and adolescents.

Prearranged. Planned ahead.

Prescribe. To write directions for the preparation and use of a medicine.

Professional. A person with training and credentials such as a degree or license in a particular area.

Proofreading. Checking over written work for errors in spelling, punctuation, capitalization, and grammar.

Psychiatrist. A medical doctor who specializes in helping people who are having difficulties with their feelings or behaviors. This doctor can also prescribe medication.

Psychologist. A doctor who talks with people to help them understand their thoughts, feelings, and behaviors. Some psychologists also do testing to learn more about people so they can help them.

Questionnaire. A form containing questions that people answer to provide information.

Receptors. Sites on a brain cell (neuron) that receive messages in the form of neurotransmitters from other brain cells.

Resource Teacher. A special education teacher who works with children individually or in small groups.

Relay System. A system in the subcortex of the brain that coordinates information coming in from the brain stem and sends it to the cerebral cortex and other parts of the brain.

Research Studies. Experiments conducted by scientists to learn about what causes certain conditions and what works best to make these conditions better.

Scans. Special pictures taken of the brain.

Social Worker. A professional who works with children and their families to help them solve their problems.

Spansule. A type of pill that delivers medication over a longer period of time.

Spell-Check. A program for the computer or small, hand-held machine that is used to find and correct spelling mistakes.

Subcortex. The area of the brain below and surrounded by the cerebral cortex.

Synapse. An extremely small space between two brain cells (neurons) that can be seen only with a microscope. Neurons send messages to each other across synapses.

Theories. Explanations that have not yet been proved to be true.

Therapist. A professional who works with children and adults to solve problems, understand feelings, or change behavior. A therapist can be a psychologist, counselor, social worker, or psychiatrist.

Transporter System. A system of proteins in the brain that carry chemicals across the cell membranes. When a brain cell releases a neurotransmitter into a synapse, the transporter system is responsible for taking the neurotransmitter back into the cell that released it.

Tutor. A person who works with children outside of class to help them learn to do better in school. A tutor may help with a particular subject area, such as math, or learning in general.

Books About AD/HD

Caffrey, Jaye. *First Star I See*. Fairport, NY: Verbal Images Press, 1997. (800-888-4741)

Carpenter, Phyllis, and Marti Ford. *Sparky's Excellent Misadventures: My ADD Journal, By Me (Sparky)*. Washington, DC: Magination Press, 2000. (800-374-2721)

Cummings, Rhonda, and Gary Fisher. *The School Survival Guide for Kids With Learning Differences*. Minneapolis, MN: Free Spirit, 1991. (800-735-7323)

Galvin, Matthew. *Otto Learns About His Medicine*. Washington, DC: Magination Press, 2001. (800-374-2721)

Gehret, Jeanne. *Eagle Eyes: A Child's Guide to Paying Attention (revised ed.)*. Fairport, NY: Verbal Images Press, 1991. (800-888-4741)

Gordon, Michael. *Jumpin' Johnny Get Back to Work*. DeWit, NY: GSI Publications, 1991. (315-446-4849)

Ingersoll, Barbara. *Distant Drums, Different Drummers: A Guide for Young People With ADHD*. Cape Publications, 1995.

James, Elizabeth, and Carol Barkin. *How to Be School Smart: Super Study Skills*. New York: Beech Tree Books, 1998.

Nadeau, Kathleen, and Ellen Dixon. *Learning to Slow Down and Pay Attention (2nd ed.)*. Washington, DC: Magination Press, 1997. (800-374-2721)

Nadeau, Kathleen, Ellen Dixon, and Susan Biggs. *School Strategies for ADD Teens: Guidelines for Schools, Parents, and Students, Grades 6-12*. Bethesda, MD: Advantage Books, 1993. (888-238-8588)

Nemiroff, Marc, and Jane Annunziata. *Help Is on the Way: A Child's Book About ADD*. Washington, DC: Magination Press, 1998. (800-374-2721)

Parker, Roberta. *Making the Grade: An Adolescent's Struggle With ADD*. Plantation, FL: A.D.D. Warehouse, 1992. (800-233-9273)

Quinn, Patricia. *Adolescents and ADD: Gaining the Advantage*. Washington, DC: Magination Press, 1995. (800-374-2721)

Quinn, Patricia, and Judith Stern. *The Best of "BRAKES": An Activity Book for Kids With ADD*. Washington, DC: Magination Press, 2000. (800-374-2721)

Quinn, Patricia, and Judith Stern. *The "Putting on the Brakes" Activity Book for Young People With ADHD.* Washington, DC: Magination Press, 1993. (800-374-2721)

Roberts, Barbara. *Phoebe Flower's Adventures: Phoebe's Best Best Friend.* Bethesda, MD: Advantage Books, 2001. (888-238-8588)

Roberts, Barbara. *Phoebe Flower's Adventures: Phoebe's Lost Treasure.* Bethesda, MD: Advantage Books, 1999. (888-238-8588)

Roberts, Barbara. *Phoebe Flower's Adventures: That's What Kids Are For.* Bethesda, MD: Advantage Books, 1998. (888-238-8588)

Romain, Trevor. *How to Do Homework Without Throwing Up.* Minneapolis, MN: Free Spirit, 1997. (800-735-7323)

Stern, Judith, and Uzi Ben-Ami. *Many Ways to Learn: Young People's Guide to Learning Disabilities.* Washington, DC: Magination Press, 1996. (800-374-2721)

Organizational Materials

"Organizational Tools for Students in Grades 3-12." Catalog available from Success by Design, 3741 Linden Ave., Wyoming, MI 49548; phone: (800) 327-0057. This catalog of useful materials for students contains items such as structured assignment notebooks and calendars.

Organizations

Children and Adults with Attention Deficit Disorder (CHADD), 8181 Professional Place, Suite 201, Landover, MD 20785; phone: (800) 233-4050; website address: www.chadd.org.

National Attention Deficit Disorder Association, 1788 Second St., Suite 200, Highland Park, IL 60035; phone: (847) 432-5874; website address: www.add.org.

Editor: Darcie Conner Johnston. Art Director: Susan K. White. The sources for the photographs and illustrations are as follows: Front cover, page 43: © Digital Vision Ltd. "Kids Stuff" group. Pages 10, 26: Nova Development Corporation, "Art Explosion 125,000 Images" group. Pages 15-17, 19, 23, 28, 30-32, 34, 36, 38, 40, 47, 51, 60, 68: © 1999 PhotoDisc, Inc. "Education 2" group. Pages 14, 18, 20, 24, 44, 48, 54, 67: © 1999 Eyewire, Inc. "Educational Concepts" group. Page 49: © 1995 Corel Corporation, "People at Work" group. Pages 52-53: © 1995 PhotoDisc, Inc. "The Object Series: Visual Symbols Sampler" group. Pages 62, 65-66: © 1999 Eyewire, Inc. "School Days" group.